We're Adopted, So What?

Teens Tell It Like It Is

**GAYLE SWIFT
with
CASEY SWIFT**

ILLUSTRATED by WESLEY BLAUVELT

We're Adopted, So What?
© 2019 by Gayle Swift

All rights reserved. No part of this publication may be reproduced, stored in a retrieval system or transmitted in any form by any means electronic, mechanical, photocopying, recording or otherwise, except brief extracts for the purpose of reviews, without the permission of the publisher and copyright owner.

Illustrations by Wesley Blauvelt

IngramSpark Publishing

www.GIFTfamilyservices.com

**Dedicated
To my beloved children,
Casey and Parker.
To all adopted children and everyone who loves them.**

Table of Contents

1. Good Things About Being Adopted
2. Things That Don't Make Sense
3. Things I Worry About
4. Things I Wish I Knew
5. Things That Bug Me About Adoption
6. It's Not Fair!
7. Hurtful Things People Ask Us
8. Things I Wish Parents Understood
9. The Scoop On Lying
10. What's The Deal With Race?
11. Things I Dislike About Myself
12. Open Adoption...
13. Quiz Time!

Madison: I was born with only one leg. I have a prosthesis but I can do ANYTHING everyone else can. I have two moms.

Sofia: I was born in Guatemala, moved to the USA when I was 2 years old. I entered foster care when I was 3 and was adopted when I was 5 years old. I have 1 older and 1 younger adopted brother who are both African-American.

Macy: I was adopted by my foster parents with my biological brothers who are much older than I am. We all get along really well.

Summer

I was born in South Korea and adopted at 18 months old. My mom is white. My dad is African-American and Chinese. I have a younger sister who was also adopted from Korea - Although she is not my biological sister.

Stefani

I was adopted at birth. My twin brother was also adopted. My birth mother was really young when she gave birth to us.

Good Things about being Adopted

 Support and Love ❤️

Brothers!

 Safety & Sisters!

Parents who love and care for us 👨‍👩‍👧

 Security

Not So Good Things about being Adopted

Unanswered Questions 🤔

Rejection

Unknown Health

Embarrassment

Anger

Things that don't make sense

If our birth parents planned adoption for us because they loved us, why didn't they love us enough to keep us?

To kids it looks like adults have all they need. Unfortunately, that isn't always true. When birth parents' problems are bigger than their available resources, they choose adoption to provide a safe, loving, and permanent home for their children.

We feel disloyal to our adoptive parents when we think about our birth parents.

Just like parents love all their children, its okay to love all the family you have. Let your adoptive parents know they are forever in your heart and that you also care for your birth parents.

People think our families aren't "real" because we are not all biologically related.

This usually happens because people don't know the correct words. They are mixing up "real" with birth family. Teach them adoption-savvy vocabulary. All your relationships, whether through birth or adoption, are real.

Why do people make fun of us for being adopted?

Adoption is the exception--most kids live with their birth families--but making fun of you is bullying. It's unfair and inappropriate. Avoid letting them know it bugs you as this usually encourages kids to keep teasing. If your efforts don't work, tell an adult.

Things We worry about

"The facts of your adoption story belong to you but some of the information may be hard to know. Your parents may tell you pieces as you are ready to learn and understand" - Stefani

Do our parents love their biological kids more than us?

Parents love all their kids. They may feel more "in tune" with some of their kids than other and have more shared interests.

We wonder if they even want us?

When we misbehave, do they wish they'd never adopted us?

Nobody enjoys conflict but parents understand that growing up is complicated. They know you will make mistakes, have disagreements, and occasionally misbehave.

Maybe you should just give us back!!

I think my parents feel hurt when I want to talk about the "hard" about adoption but I need help facing it. I'm torn with wanting to protect them and being angry that I have to worry about them. I need them to love me enough to walk through it with me. What if it is too much for them?

It is painful for parents to see their kids struggle but it is important to handle these issues as a family even if it is hard for all of you. If you can't say it out loud, try writing your ideas and concerns down. And remember empathy and reassurance helps everyone.

Things We Wish We Knew

How big will we grow?

Your doctor might be able to predict how tall you will be from your growth rate patterns or information about your birth parents.

Does she look like us?

Do we have any biological brothers or sisters?

You can ask your parents to look in your records. Some birth parents do have other children. They may have been born before or after you were adopted. If your adoption is closed, the answer may be unavailable.

We wonder if we'd be friends...

BFF

Why were we adopted?

This may be a great question to ask your birth parents or you can talk with your parents about what they know. One thing is certain: you did not cause your adoption. It is not your fault. Your birth parents did not have the skills, health, or resources to safely raise you. The specific problems will vary from person to person, adoption to adoption. But the reasons are BIG not simple things that could be easily fixed.

notebook:

Things that bug us about Adoption:

"People stare at my family because we look so different." - Summer

Nobody likes to feel like a science project on display but people do notice when families obviously don't "match". Decide if you want to ignore or confront folks. Respond with courtesy or humor. Their stares and whispers are their problem not yours. Don't allow them to dump their "stuff" on you.

"People asking personal questions and expecting me to answer." - Stefani

Answer only the questions you want. Be cautious about what and with whom you share your private business. Avoid over-sharing. Once you've shared information, it can't be taken back. Some people won't respect your privacy and some people might use information to bully you.

"School projects like family trees and family history stuff make me feel weird." - Macy

Being adopted complicates some projects. Let your teacher know if an assignment makes you uncomfortable. You--or your parents can explain to your teacher why the project is challenging for you. Ask for an alternative assignment. If you want, you can choose either your adoptive family, birth family, or both.

"Why can't I just be a kid instead of 'The adopted kid'?" - Madison

Nobody likes to be labeled. Let people know they are being rude and hurtful. Sometimes when people don't understand things, they can be insensitive. Adoption is puzzling to people who aren't adopted. (Heck, it can be pretty confusing even if you are adopted!) When you feel up to it, help people learn-share your thoughts and feelings. When you need more privacy, let people know they have over-stepped.

"Why do people think I should forget my birth parents?" - Sofia

It isn't easy to explain to "outsiders" how you can love your adoptive family so much and still love/think/care about your birth family. Most adoptees do think about their birth family. It is okay! They are both an important part of your life story.

It's NOT Fair!

Our siblings talk to their birth families but we don't even have a picture.

Yup, some things are not fair so...
– Own the feelings and move on.
– Change what is unfair-if possible.
– Picture her based on the information you do have.

notebook:

Our adoption is closed...why didn't she want to get to know us?

"Closed" adoptions-when kids have no contact with their birth family occur because of adult problems. They are absolutely not the child's fault. Even if your adoption is "closed," you may still be able to obtain more information. Ask your parents directly. (Now that you're older, they maybe willing to share more information--if they have it.) Or, have them request additional facts from the agency, attorney, or orphanage that handled your adoption.

All our non-adopted friends seem to have perfect little lives with nothing wrong...Why us?

Things may look perfect in other families but usually they are not. Perfect families are usually just on TV. In all families, parents set rules. Some are more strict than others, but remember they are parents first and friends second.

Seek out other adoptees. They share the same thoughts, feelings, and experiences. They'll understand you because they're facing the same kind of stuff.

People often talk and ask questions without thinking. Remember this:

1. You do not owe them an answer.
2. Most people are unaware of the messy reality of being adopted.

Try this:

Respond to hurtful questions with humor, ignoring them, or answer with other questions: Why do you want to know?

notebook:

Things We wish our parents understood

You can't just "fix" how we feel.

Just because we say we don't think about our adoption doesn't mean adoption doesn't affect us. We may even be hoping you will talk about it to prove it really is a permissable topic.

Sometimes we yell at you, even though we are mad at someone else.

We might try to test your limits to see how far we can push you, just to remind us that you love us no matter what. One of our deepest fears is that we might cause you to give us back.

notebook:

We might get angry and say hurtful things.

When we get really angry, we might yell, "You can't tell me what to do because you're not my real mom." We don't mean it and we're sorry. We're feeling overwhelmed by our big emotions.

Sometimes we want to ask questions about our adoption but we are afraid that it will hurt you.

Our adoptive families and our birth families are a part of us. When people speak about them disrespectfully, it hurts our feelings.

The scoop on lying

Sometimes we invent stuff about ourselves, even with our friends. We're scared they won't like the "real us."

Lying teaches people not to like or trust you because lying shows you don't even like yourself. The first person you must convince that the "real" you is great is...YOU! Many adoptees feel rejection, blame, and shame about being adopted. These feelings cloud the way they feel about themselves. Remember adoption is not your fault. Sometimes it does feel good to make up stories to make yourself look better. But most of the time, your friends can see right through the lies. Instead of telling people what you think they want to hear, find ways that you can shine and still be you.

notebook:

When you feel a constant need to make yourself look or sound better than you feel you are, take a step back. Study people. Which folks make you feel "not good enough"? Are those people that you really want to be around? You deserve friends who like you for who you are, and not some made up version of yourself. Find ways to encourage your friends to be themselves around you. The more they feel safe being themselves around you, the safer and easier it will be for you to be real with them.

Instead of lying, work to become a person you can be proud of. Decide what you want to change then work to make those changes true. Lying shows you don't trust people with your truth. What would it take to trust more? What would your friends need to do or say to convince you they are trustworthy? Make a list of all the times your friends were there when you needed them. Do they measure up? If not, you might want to find friends who value the real you.

Imagine your very best friend listed all the great things she knows about you, what would she mention? Now actually ask your BFFs to tell you one thing they like about you. Keep a list of their answers. Yes, they will have some great things to say. Why else would they be your friend? Be the kind of friend you need and want. Start by being a good friend to yourself.

What's the Deal with Race?

Race confuses us. Do we have to choose one race or the other?

Race is a core part of who you are. It is permanent, something you can't change. When people treat you with prejudice and don't accept you, it hurts. It can be confusing when people say they do not "see" your race. They intend to be comforting but it shows a blind spot about a very important part of you. Let them know you want them to appreciate your race instead of denying it.

If you have parents of a different race or if you are multi-racial, things can be even more complicated. While adoption affects you most directly, it is a family experience. Each of you is influenced by this racial diversity. You may wonder where you fit in, or if you will ever fit in. Meet many people and make friends. Read books and stories that include and respect diverse characters and cultures. Clue your parents in about what works and what doesn't. Don't keep them guessing. Mind reading is unreliable!

If people treat you with prejudice when your white, or racially dissimilar parents are not with you, let your folks know. You need their support. Parents want to ensure that people respect you. As transracial parents, they are committed for the rest of their lives to educate people about race and to insist on racial equality. Don't tolerate discrimination. Stand up for yourself and for your family. Remember, attitude counts. Be firm but respectful.

Things we dislike about ourselves

I look so different from the rest of my family

It is fun to choose to look or be different, but it can be very uncomfortable when the difference is some-thing you can't change about yourself, imagine a crayon box with only one color. Pretty dull, right? Learn to love what's different about yourself. It is what makes you unique. Be the rainbow instead of the grey cloud.

notebook:

struggle in school. (I'm creative but math... OMG!)

Parents expect kids to do their best in school. For some kids, that means achieving high grades. For others, grades may not reflect the earnest effort they have exerted. The important thing is to work hard. Diffficult doesn't mean impossible. Achieving challenging goals feels good.

Open Adoption is supposed to make things easier but...

Every Goodbye is hard. Yet we value and appreciate these visits.

"Sometimes I get really angry with my birth mom. Why did she have to give me up? I feel so disappointed if she has to cancel a visit. I love my birth mom's kids but I'm jealous that they get to grow up with her. I care about what my birth mom thinks and says but I don't want her to tell me what to do." - Stefani

Why them, and not me?

Circle the response that fits you best!

1. If I were an animal, I would be

    A. A chameleon – I blend in with any group
    B. An eagle – I like to excel and take risks
    C. A dog – Everyone can read my moods
    D. A mouse – I'm timid and very cautious
    E. An ostrich – I ignore stuff and hide my head

2. If I were a color, I would be

- A. White - I fade into the background
- B. Red - I love to stand out
- C. Blue - Like clean water, and fresh air, people enjoy when I'm around
- D. Yellow - I make people smile
- E. Grey - I feel sad a lot

3. If I were a song, I would be

- A. A lullaby - I'm so gentle and quiet, people don't even notice me
- B. A rap song - I have a lot on my mind & I shout it out
- C. A march - I know what I want and go for it
- D. A jingle - I convince people to follow me
- E. An opera - I LOVE drama

4. If I were a dessert, I would be

- A. A vanilla Pudding - I pair well with lots of fruits
- B. A candy bar - A bit nutty, a bit sweet
- C. A popsicle - I melt when things get "hot"
- D. A warhead candy - Sour and feisty
- E. A cupcake - Attractive on the outside, all crumbly inside

5. If I were a shoe, I would be

- A. A pair of slippers - comfy and ready to relax
- B. A sneaker - I'm strong and steady
- C. Flip-flop - I fall apart easily when things get "rough"
- D. A boot - I have a hard, tough exterior
- E. High heels - I look good on the outside, but it hurts to do it

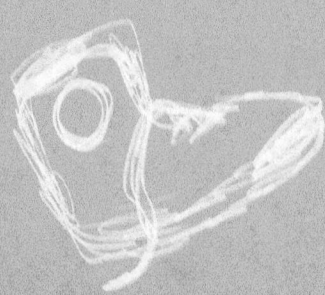

6. If my family were a band, I'd play

   A. Piano - complex, loud and soft, warm and cool
   B. Kettle drum - when I speak everyone listens
   C. Flute - I'm sweet and lively
   D. Bass guitar - everybody marches to my beat
   E. Cymbals - I'm dramatic and like to get my way

7. If my family was a team, we'd play

   A. Softball - we each know our assigned positions
   B. Swimming - we each have a speciality and work together
   C. Soccer - we get out our feelings by kicking the ball around
   D. Dance - we each have a special flair
   E. Basketball - we're constantly running and playing defense

8. If I were a season, I'd be

A. Indian Summer - a bit of every season's weather

B. Summer - I bring warmth to my family and friends

C. Autumn - I can blow hot and cold

D. Spring - I bring life to the party

E. Winter - I can be gorgeous and cold at the same time

9. If I were a number, I'd be

A. Zero - nobody notices me

B. One - I like myself and I'm comfortable alone

C. Two - I need to be with a friend

D. Seven - I'm a lucky person

E. Ten - I prefer a crowd

10. If I were a spice, I'd be

    A. Sugar – People are glad when I'm around

    B. Salt – I add a dash of excitement

    C. Pepper – I keep the heat up

    D. Cinnamon – I'm sweet and spicy

    E. Curry – I bring an exotic, international flavor

11. If I were a drink, I'd be

    A. Water – everyone needs to drink me

    B. Chocolate milk – I'm sweet, and comforting

    C. Soda – I'm bubbly and sweet

    D. Coffee – my energy fires up everybody else

    E. Ice tea with lemon – I'm a mix of sweet and sour

12. If I were weather, I'd be

A. Sunny - says it all, everyone likes to have me around

B. Rain shower - I cry easily and then feel much better

C. Tornado - I let nothing get in the way of my plans

D. Hurricane - I'm loud, moody and a force to deal with

E. Blizzard - I'm cold, pushy and like to cover things up

13. If my life story were a book, it would be

A. Comedy - I make people laugh

B. Adventure - learning to beat the challenges

C. Mystery - so many unanswered questions

D. Science Fiction - a medical miracle

E. Tragedy - so many bad things have happened

14. If I were clothing, I would be

A. Jeans - I'm adaptable and work with everything

B. A bikini - I let people see the real me

C. A sweater - I like to snuggle and be warm and cozy

D. A Sundress - I show myself, keeping the important parts private

E. An overcoat - I like to cover things up

15. When talking about my adoption I am

A. A muted microphone - I keep my thoughts to myself

B. An open book - what you see is what you get

C. A locked safe - only I know what I'm thinking and feeling

D. A song that never ends - I'll talk as long as you'll listen

E. A sealed envelope - I'm just waiting for you to act, to ask...

What did you notice?

If you chose mostly

A: You change to fit people's expectations.
B: You are clear about what you want.
C: You share your ideas and feelings easily.
D: You like a lot of control.
E: You hide what is really on your mind.

Help Yourself Communicate Better

Keep a journal.

Talk it out with a trustworthy friend. Discuss stuff with your parents as if it were happening to a friend. Express it through art – music, drawing, etc. Write it as a "story" and share it with your folks.

What are some of the best things about being adopted?

_____
_____
_____
_____
_____
_____
_____

Are there any not-so-great things?

_____
_____
_____
_____
_____
_____

What questions do you have?

What makes you worry?

What things do you wish your parents understood?

What "bugs" you?

FRIENDS

FRIENDS

How to talk about the "hard stuff" with your parents.

1. Look for an uninterrupted time to talk, like a car ride to school, or a trip to the Grocery store.

2. Start with a question.

3. Share how you feel.

4. Give examples of how they can help.

5. Don't be afraid to share emotions.

THE END

Authors and Illustrator

Award-winning author Gayle H. Swift drew on her experience as an adoptive parent, adoption coach and foster parent to create **We're Adopted, So What?** Co-founder of GIFT Family Services, she is dedicated to supporting adoptees and the families who love them.

Casey Anne Swift, adoptee, teacher, and co-author of **We're Adopted, So What?**, collaborated with her mother on this project. Together, they have created a book designed to support and encourage adoptees as they travel their adoption journey.

Wesley Blauvelt, illustrated and designed **We're Adopted, So What?**. Wesley enjoyed collaborating with both authors to bring the message of love, acceptance and understanding to support adoptees and their families. Wesley also created and illustrated the **Andy Biotic** health education series of children's books.

"This is a treasure and will help so many families. I love this book so much. I wish I'd had it when my kids were younger."

Lori Holden, author of *The Open-hearted Way to Open Adoption*

"My hope is that prospective adoptive parents will buy and read this book before they become parents. Good adoptive parenting requires you to first seek to understand your child's perspective. Owning this book is a good first step."

Lynn Grubb, adoptee and kinship adoptive parent, editor and creator of *The Adoptee Survival Guide*

If you enjoyed this book, please consider posting a review on Amazon.

Titles Available for Children

*revised and reillustrated book *original award-winning book

"Reading this book with your children is a great way to address sensitive questions and issues around the subject of adoption. This book promotes acceptance and understanding of adoption in a loving way!"
Carle Sargent, Founder and President - US Adoption Solutions, Inc., Author-
The Family Zoo

ABC, Adoption & Me is anadorable, early readers adoption book written by Gayle Swift. *ABC, Adoption & Me* uses the alphabet to introduce various adoption related concepts to childern. The book provides parents the opportunity to open difficult conversations with their child, educate their child about adoption, and improve their child's self esteem. As an adoption therapist, I recommend every family have a copy of *ABC, Adoption & Me* for their young child.
Carol Lozier, MSW, LCSW
Author of *The Adoptive & Foster Parent Guide*

Titles Available for Adults

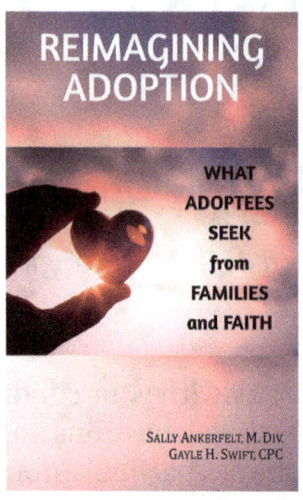

"*Reimagining Adoption*" examines beliefs, practices, and Scripture to distill adoption policy steeped in Christian values and attuned to the needs of vulnerable children and their families.

"*This book opens people of faith to a different perspective than what you would normally hear in mainstream media, your church and your community about adoption. Share it with your pastor, your congregation, and other people of faith.*" – **Lynn Grubb, Adoptee, Kinship Adoptive Parent. Editor,** ***The Adoptee Survival Guide***

"Talking with co-author, Sally, was cathartic. I have been grappling with how faith intersects with cultural identity and family dynamics. Talking about my journey was healing and thought-provoking. Sharing my story and reading a book that uses real voices, real words, and real experiences validated my own experience. This book elevated my faith. It is a rare find."
– Lolita, fosteree, child welfare professional

www.ingramcontent.com/pod-product-compliance
Lightning Source LLC
Chambersburg PA
CBHW052119070526
44584CB00017B/2564